First Edition, 2021

Tonya A. Brown
3436 Magazine St
#460
New Orleans, LA 70115
www.witchwaypublishing.com

Writer and Editor: Tonya A. Brown
Internal Design: Amanda Smith
Cover Design: Katie McCay
Special Thanks: Amanda Wilson, Kiki Dombrowski, Nyx "Spence" Spencer, Lilith Cotton, Tammy Hill, Hollie Eaddy-Kohvakka, and Casey Otto

Printed in the United States of America

ISBN 978-1087915630

EVOLUTION OF A WITCH

150 Journal Prompts for Witches

TONYA A. BROWN

IF LOST, PLEASE RETURN TO:

How to use this Journal

This book is a prompt journal meant to be reflective and enjoyable. While some questions will ask you to ponder your practices and your beliefs, others will simply ask you to think creatively about life and the world around you.

This journal is not meant to be completed in one sitting. Instead, it is intended to encourage you to think more deeply about questions that, on the surface, could seem simple. We recommend that you complete this journal slowly, either working on one question per day, or even one per week.

USE THIS JOURNAL TO:

- Think more deeply about the world around you
- Start discussions with friends and family
- Find topics to use during meditation
- Curate topics to be used in classes or panels
- Find ideas for other creative works
- Elaborate further on your other journals or notebooks

Remember to leave judgment behind. We cannot grow and evolve if we are afraid to look at ourselves in a deep and critical way. Be gentle and kind to yourself as you do.

Using your intuition, how do you predict your life is going to change this year?

What is one memory from last year you hope that you never forget?

Explore the psychic clairs! Clairvoyance, Clairgustance, Claircognizance, Clairsentience, Clairalience, and Clairaudience. Which one are you? How many do you possess?

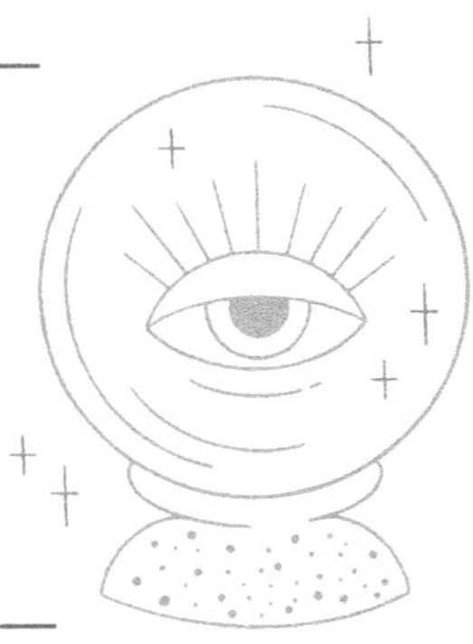

Hear no evil, speak no evil, see no evil, and do no evil. Pick one. Why did you choose this one?

What spirit or deity is calling to you right now? If there isn't one, take this opportunity to write down what you're looking for in a spiritual familiar.

Who do you look up most to and why? What about this person inspires you?

Do you believe in soulmates? Why or why not? Are they purely romantic? Can you have more than one? Do you think we choose this person?

Do you need to update your routine? If so, do it here! If not, what about your routine works for you?

If you could have one superpower what would it be? Is it practical or just for fun? What would you use it for?

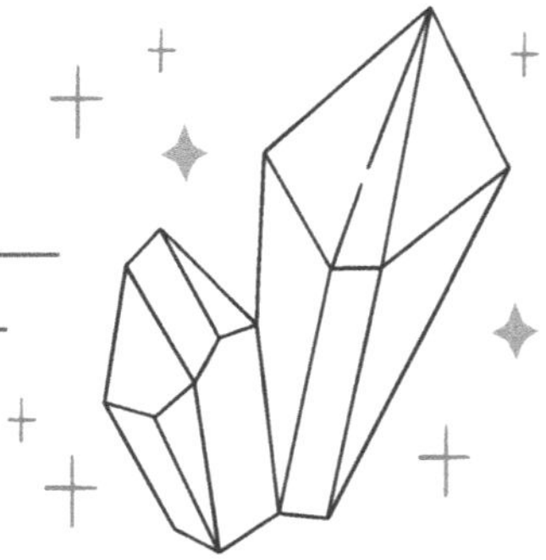

What is the biggest lesson you've learned so far in life? How has it changed your view of yourself or the world?

What element do you most relate to and why? Fire, Earth, Air, Water, or Spirit?

How did you develop your altar? Why is it set up the way that it is? If you do not use an altar, how do you set up your magical space?

What was the best day you had this week? What made it so lovely? What aspects would you want to integrate into your everyday?

When was the last time you've taken a leap of faith? How did it turn out? Did you trust your instincts?

Do you currently feel blessed or cursed? Explain.

What is your favorite witch movie? What about it makes it your favorite?

What would you consider to be your magical niche? Do you want to hone in on it further or branch out?

Do you currently have a talisman or good luck charm? What is it and how did it come to you?

What are your favorite scents and scent combos? Don't have one? Start exploring!

What is one spell that you know by heart? Share it here. Explain how you came to it.

What are some recent headlines and how do you feel about them? Are you feeling empowered within the current world?

What was the last magical item you purchased? How did you use it or plan to use it?

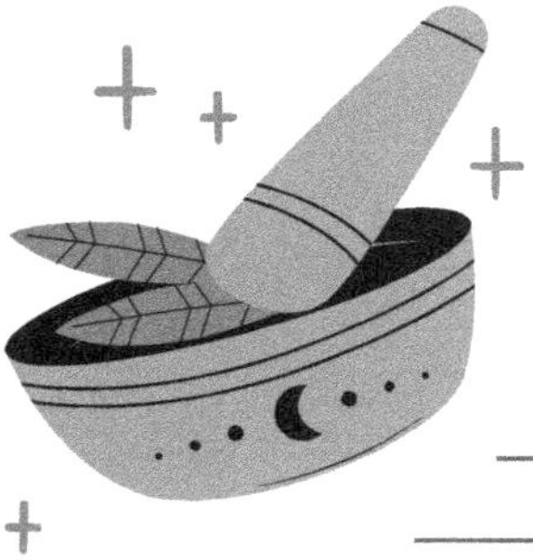

If your life was a book, what would the title be and w
the chapters be named up to this point in your life?

Wr

Which is more powerful? Fate or free will? Can we change fate? Does free will trump all?

Who is the most magical person you know and why did you choose them? Do they rub off on you or you on them?

What is your most believed in superstition? What about it makes it so powerful within your life? Where did you learn it?

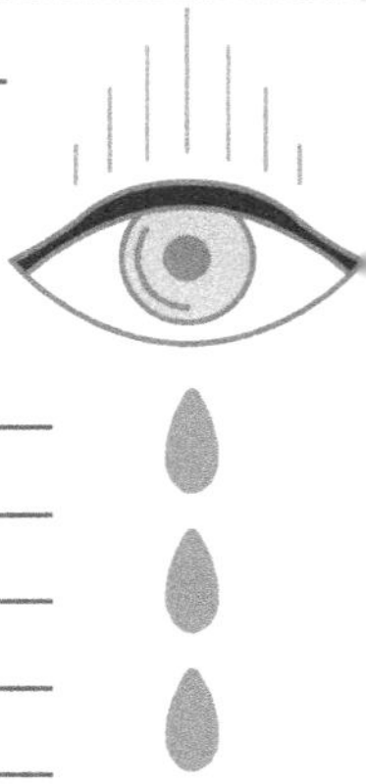

What rituals in your life make you most happy?
Are they mundane or magical?

If you could be the best at anything, what would it be? How would you use this skill in your life?

Predict what will happen this week:

My last successful spell was:
It brought me:

My last unsuccessful spell was:

It taught me:

What gets you through a hard day? Do you need to find new ways to cope or can you make this one more accessible?

Do you have anything to confess? If so, how do you plan to grow from this?

Favorite magical book right now? What is it about? What makes it stand out?

Favorite magical podcast right now? Is it relaxing and fun or thoughtful and dense? If you don't have one, how would you format a magical radio show?

What did you eat today? Was this routine or an exploration? Is it time to shake up your taste buds?

Are you happy with your magical community? What do you like most about it? What would you change?

Coffee or tea? Do you consume them differently? Is one more spiritual than the other?

Do you have a book of shadows or a grimoire? If so how do you arrange and organize them?

What 3 items would be used to summon you?
Are they unique to you or would it relate to many?

Coven, solitary, or both? How does community and connectedness relate to your magical practice?

Do you always trust your instincts? What happened the last time you listened to your gut?

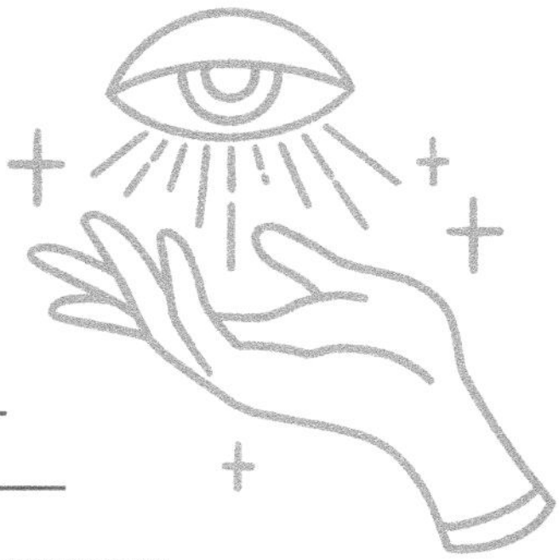

If you could make one wish right now, what would it be? How do you see this playing out in your life?

Waning or waxing? Which moon phase do you find yourself using the most? If you do not use moon phases, do you feel your life wanes or waxes?

Who would be in your ideal coven? (You can add celebrities, we totally will not judge you.)

What do you dream about? Either in your fantasties or while you are sleeping.

Do you regret any spells? What happened that caused you to second guess your choices? How would you act differently?

If you were a deity, what colors, flowers, foods, and offerings would be related to you? Do you have an invocation?

Do you think your home is haunted? If so, who is there? How do you live alongside the entity?

Where do you think you'll be in 5 years?
Is this what you want?

What is the last dream you remember? Who or what was in it? What emotions were present in it? Was it enjoyable?

What is the most expensive magical item you own? Share how you obtained it. Was it worth the money?

What life lesson do you struggle to learn? Are there patterns in your life you struggle to break free from?

Name a form of divination that you would like to learn more about. Summarize it here. Make action steps to explore it.

List out your current ritual or go-to spellwork steps. What about it works well for you?

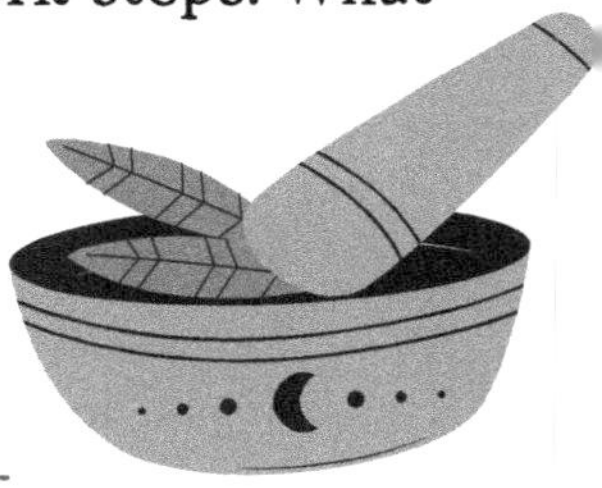

If you could rename yourself, what would you call yourself and why? Would it be a public name or a private one?

Pull three cards right now, what is the reading? List what deck you used and the cards pulled so you can reflect on it later.

Plan your perfect day below. No restrictions.

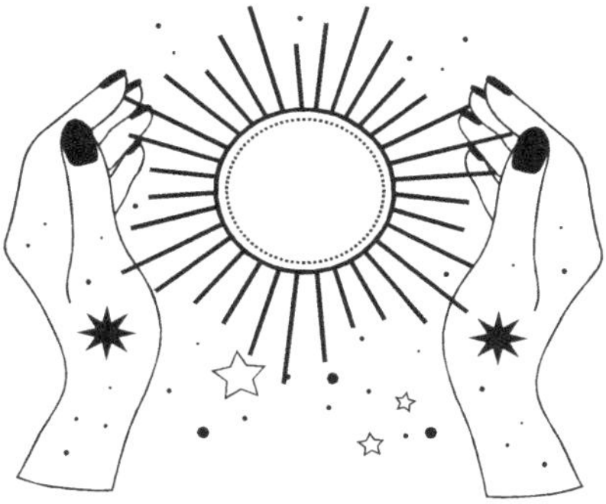

Do you follow the wheel of the year? If so, what is your favorite holiday? If not, define what would be your perfect celebration.

What is one thing you want to do before you cross over? Do you have a plan to get there?

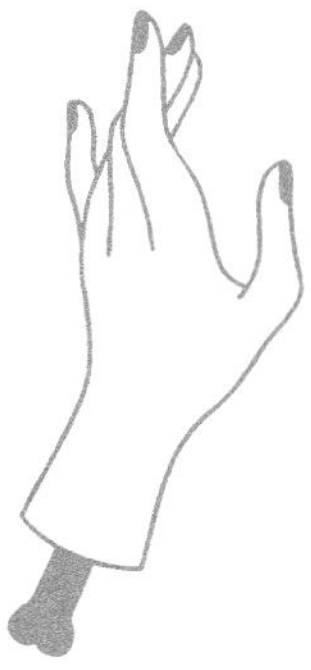

If you could know anything, what would it be? Mysteries? Languages? Information?

Who or what experiece has shaped your life the most? Would you ever choose to undo this experience?

Think of a time you felt powerful, and describe what occurred to bring you to that moment.

Do you believe in the Rule of Three? If so, why? If not, do you think it holds any credence?

What is your personal magical philosophy? How has it changed over the years? Is it in need of an update?

If you could read other people's thoughts, would you? How would you use this skill in your daily life?

What is something that worked in your favor today? Was it a surprise or something you had set in motion?

What are some daily rituals that make you happy? What are other small things you can add to bring you joy?

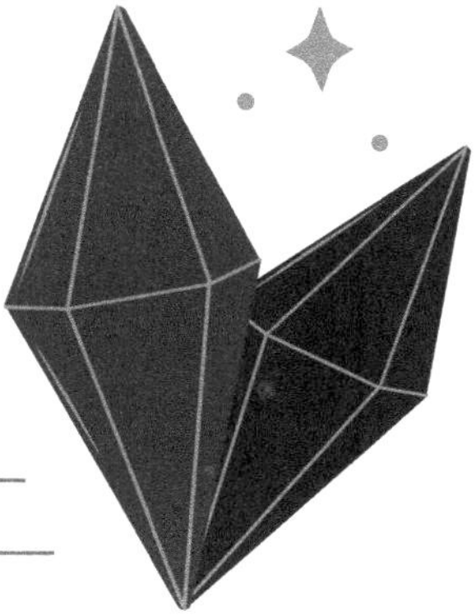

If you could be perfect at something, what would that thing be and why? How would it change your life?

I am :

Complete the sentence. There is no wrong direction here.

To curse or not to curse?

What is the overall theme of your magical practice? What are patterns you recycle in your spellwork or craft?

If you could be a fly on the wall during any historical event, what event would you witness and why?

What is your favorite time of day/day of the week/season? How do these times make you feel?

What is your least favorite time of day/day of the week/season? What do you do during these unfavorable times to bring in joy and power?

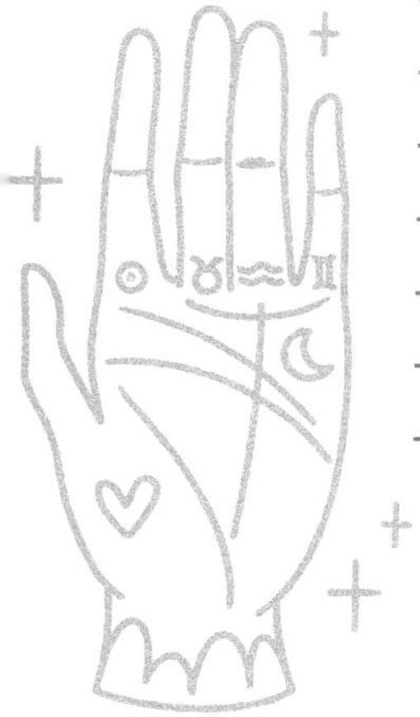

Do you celebrate all of your big wins? If not make a plan to do so here.

Talk about another witch in your life. Explain them as if they were a fictional character.

To Ouija, or not to Ouija?
Have you had any unbelievable divinatory experiences?

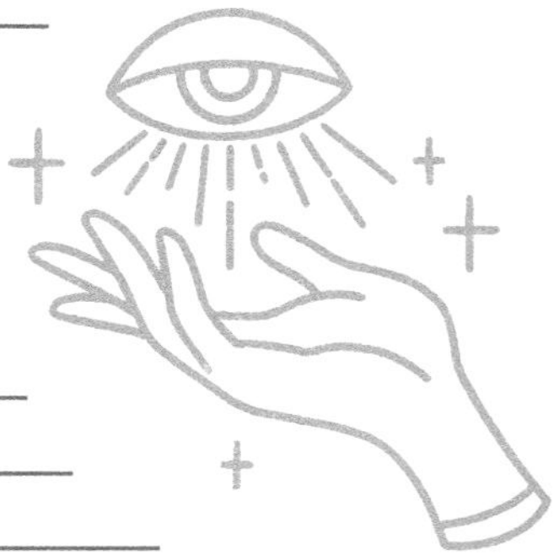

If you could get advice from a fictional witch, who would it be? What would you ask them? What would they tell you?

Are you happy? How can you continue or change this?

What do you seek on the path that you are on? Why?

Share here some life advice that you've learned through your hardest experiences.

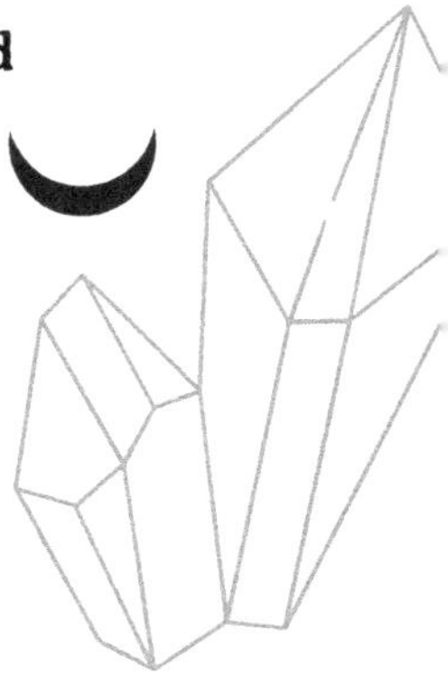

What is your favorite quote at the moment? Why does it speak to you?

If you could live as someone else for a week, who would it be and why?

If you could cast a spell and get instant results, what would you cast?

What is one magical practice or act you would never perform and why?

What are some fears you have? What brought these fears along? Do you need to challenge them?

Do you like Halloween? What is your favorite Halloween costume? Is it spooky, empowering, silly, or all three?

Do you work with spirits? How do you currently connect to them and how do you want to grow this relationship?

How do you want to be remembered?

Do you plan to pass on your magic or traditions? If so, to who? How are you gathering information for them now?

If you could tell your younger self something, what would it be? Would your younger self listen?

What is your favorite crystal or tool? How did it become you favorite and how do you use it

Is there such thing as a good deed? What was the last good deed you did?

Who would play you in a movie? What would the plot be?

Do you have a solid support system?
Are you a strong presence for someone else?

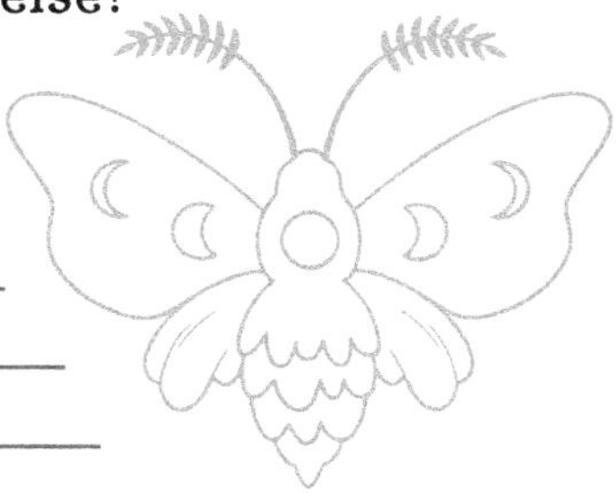

Is there a song that speaks to your soul? What are the lyrics?

Press your hands to your scalp. Run your hands down over your skin. What tension is there?

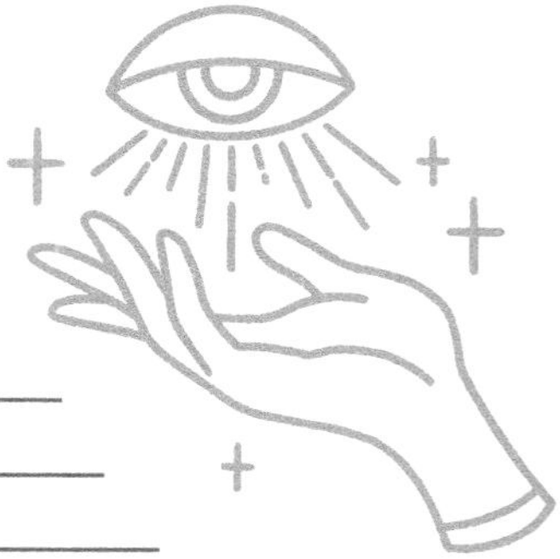

If you could ask a deceased family member one question, what would it be and why would their answer be important?

Thinking about the history of magic, what are a few things the scholars got right, and things they got wrong?

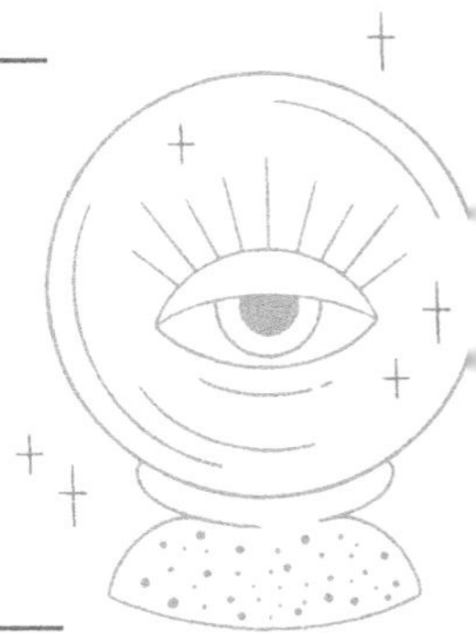

If you could control your dreams, what would you choose to dream about?

List the places that you long to go and the reasons why. What is an action plan to help you get to one of those places?

Think about and list things that made your childhood magical. Do you still view the world the same? In what ways has your perspective changed?

What is your first memory of a spiritual experience? How does it make you feel now?

If you could plan a magical course catalog what are some of the classes that would be offered?

If you were able to safely visit the Otherworld, what would you do while you were there?

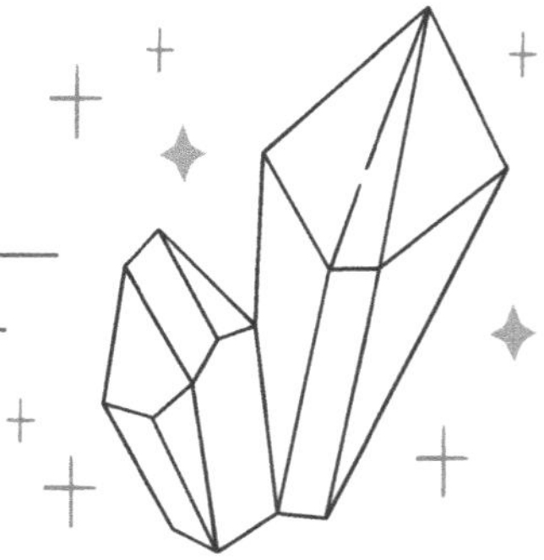

If you could make a spell book out of songs, which songs would you include and why?

Describe a place, real or imaginary, that you consider to be a magical and sacred location. Where is it and how do you feel there?

What was the first magical item you ever owned? How did you get it? Do you still use it?

What is your favorite tarot or oracle card? How does it speak to you and why did it become your favorite?

A Tarot deck and an Oracle Deck took human form and got into a fight. Describe the highlights and who won.

What is one change you would make that you believe would make the world a better place?

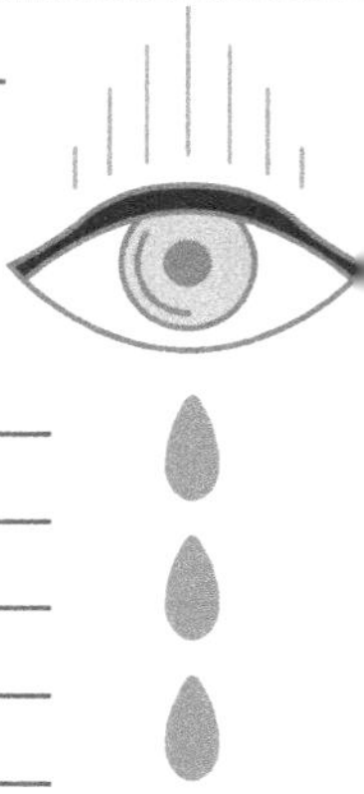

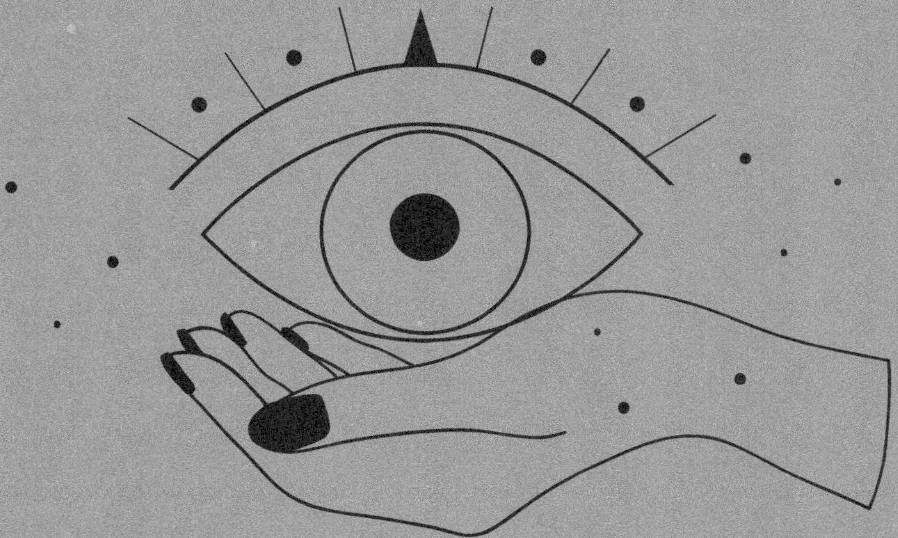

What is your favorite magical herb? How do you most use it and why is it your favorite?

What is your purpose? If you don't know, devise a plan to discover what it is.

If you were a fairy tale character, what character would you be? What would you change in the story?

What archetype do you most relate to? (Warrior, caretaker, student, teacher, guard, farmer, oracle, royalty, etc.) What aspects of you relate to this?

If you could adopt any mythical creature, what would you adopt? What would you name it? Where would you keep it?

If you could go forward 10 years in time to ask your future-self one question, what would you ask?

Imagine you established a new witchcraft tradition. What is it called? What is it's most notable feature? How is it different?

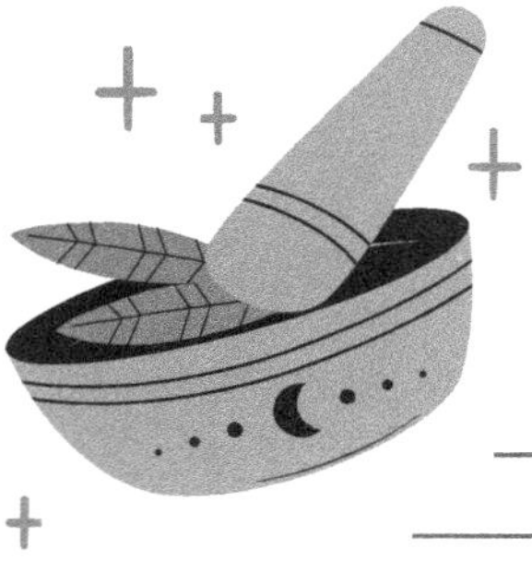

What do you feel is the most important part of a ritual? Aesthetic, chants, intention, clothing, supplies, invocation, etc?

You wake up and discover you are in a different time and place
When & where are you? What do you do there?

What is one time you felt disappointed by someone in your life? How did that change your perception of them?

Do you believe in good vs. evil? How do you think the universe stays in balance?

If you found yourself dropped in an alternate universe, who would be the first person you would seek out and why?

Describe the perfect home that fosters and nurtures you and your magical practice. What rooms would be there? Who would live there? How would it look and feel?

If you could plan and organize a magical retreat for you and th
magical people in your life, what would a day there look like?

Ritual or spellwork? Which do you feel is most important? Why did you choose the one that you did?

If you had the ability to morph into any animal or creature, which would you choose and why?

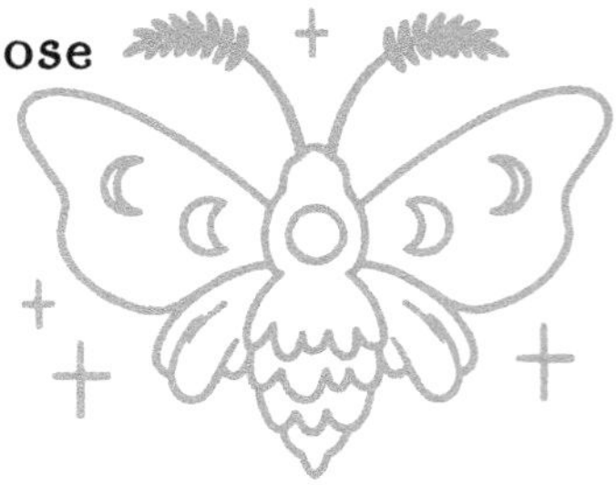

Do you feel heard and seen? Why or why not? Explore those feelings.

Do you believe in working love spells? How do you think people should navigate those magical waters?

Alcohol in spellwork and ritual? How do you use it? How do you not use it?

What is one spell that you cast that you are happy never came to manifest? What were your motivations?

If a magical secret society asked you to join, would you? What would your role be? How would it be organized?

Name a family member, who if you found out they were a witch, would not surprise you. What about their actions led you to that answer?

Do you believe in love? Do you think people only find it once? Explain.

What do you believe is the most ideal use of magic? Explain.

How do you beleive magic should never be used? Explain.

List the ways in which you and your magic benefit the people and the world around you.

If there was a witch-based television channel, what are some of the programming and series that it would offer?

If each element could tell the world one thing, what do you think they would say? Earth, Air, Fire, Water, and Spirit.

If you could see into the lives of anyone, anytime you wanted, who would you check in on and when? Why?

Have you ever astral projected? What was that experience like? If not, how would you like that experience to be?

If there was an apocalypse, do you think witches could save the world? If so, how?

What do you personally believe makes someone a witch?

Do you have a familiar? If so, share about them and how they help in your practice.

How do you hope to inspire and encourage the generation that comes after you?

Do you beleive that everyone gets their comeuppance? Do you believe that good things happen to good people?

How do you define good? What makes a behavior truly good?

If you had an entire week to yourself, how would you take advantange of that time?

Go back to the first prompt in this journal. You predicted the year. Were you correct so far?

WITCH WAY
PUBLISHING